D1173341

INTRODUCTION

Ruth Bader Ginsburg is one of our greatest progressive thinkers and a feminist folk hero. Confirmed to the Supreme Court of the United States in 1993, Ruth Bader Ginsburg has become the champion of the discerning dissent. Inspired by her objections, admirers have bestowed her with the title "Notorious R.B.G." as she continues to advocate for women and those who need to have their voices heard. This pocket-size quote book is full of insightful, inspiring, motivational, and humorous quotes Judge Ginsburg has said over the years. Proving time and time again that she is a force to be reckoned with, Ruth Bader Ginsburg will forever be an American treasure.

"Real change, enduring change, happens one step at a time."

"Reacting in anger
or annoyance will
not advance one's
ability to
persuade."

"When a thoughtless or unkind word is spoken, best tune out."

"Fight for the things that you care about, but do it in a way that will lead others to join you."

"You can't have it all, all at once."

"I'm a very strong believer in listening and learning from others."

"In the course of a marriage, one accommodates the other."

"A gender line helps to keep women not on a pedestal, but in a cage."

"If you want to be a true professional, do something outside yourself."

"Don't be distracted by emotions like anger, envy, resentment. These just zap energy and waste time."

"In every good marriage, it helps sometimes to be a little deaf."

"My mother told me two things constantly. One was to be a lady, and the other was to be independent."

"Women will have achieved true equality when men share with them the responsibility of bringing up the next generation."

"I've gotten much more satisfaction for the things that I've done for which I was not paid."

"I'm constantly amazed by the number of people who want to take my picture."

"If I had any talent in the world, I would be a great diva."

"There will be enough women on the Supreme Court when there are nine."

"We have the oldest written constitution still in force in the world, and it starts out with three words, 'We, the people.'"

"Enjoy what makes you happy, bring along your crew, have a sense of humor."

"When contemplated in its extreme, almost any power looks dangerous."

"I ask no favor for my sex. All I ask of our brethren is that they take their feet off our necks."

"I remember envying the boys long before I even knew the word feminism, because I liked shop better than cooking or sewing."

"For both men and women the first step in getting power is to become visible to others, and then to put on an impressive show."

"The law cannot apply one rule to Joe who is a good man, and another to John, who is a hardened criminal."

"Choosing the right word, and the right word order, could make an enormous difference in conveying an image or an idea."

"The state controlling a woman would mean denying her full autonomy and full equality."

"For so long women were silent, thinking there was nothing you could do about it, but now the law is on the side of women, or men, who encounter harassment and that's a good thing."

"I wish there was a way I could wave a magic wand and put back when people were respectful of each other and the Congress was working for the good of the country and not just along party lines."

"Reproductive choice has to be straightened out."

"Every woman of my vintage knows what sexual harassment is, although we didn't have a name for it."

"Someday there will be great people, great elected representatives who will say, 'enough of this nonsense, let's be the kind of legislature the United States should have.'"

"So we have a policy that affects only poor women, and it can never be otherwise, and I don't know why this hasn't been said more often."

"I am fearful, or suspicious, of generalizations. They cannot guide me reliably in making decisions about particular individuals."

"We've come a long way from the days where there was state-enforced segregation. But we still have a way to go."

"If you're going to change things, you have to be with the people who hold the levers."

"I also wanted them to see I was alive and well, contrary to that senator who said I'd be dead within nine months."

"The emphasis must be not on the right to abortion but on the right to privacy and reproductive control."

"I do a variety of weight-lifting, elliptical glider, stretching exercises, push-ups. And I do the Canadian Air Force exercises almost every day."

"I really concentrate on what's on my plate at the moment and do the very best I can."

"I would not look to the U.S. Constitution if I were drafting a constitution."

"Not a law firm in the entire city of New York bid for my employment as a lawyer when I earned my degree."

"It is not women's liberation, it is women's and men's liberation."

"People certainly know that women are present on the court. And we are all over the bench and we are certainly here to stay."

"My hope for our society that we're gonna use the talent of all of the people and not just half of them."

"I will do this job as long as I feel that I can do it full steam."

"No one who is in business for profit can foist his or her beliefs on a workforce that includes many people who do not share those beliefs."

"Just think how you would like the women in your family to be treated, particularly your daughters."

"I read every federal case that had to do with women's equality. Now that seems like it was quite an undertaking but in fact, it was easily manageable because there was so little."

"I do hope that some of my dissents will one day be the law."

"Justice Scalia and I served together on the D.C. Circuit. So his votes are not surprising to me. What I like about him is that he's very funny and very smart."

"You can imagine how exhilarating it was for me when the women's movement came alive in the late sixties and it became possible to do something about all that. Before then, you were talking to the wind."

"An operatic voice
is like no other."

"Now Kagan is on my left, and Sotomayor is on my right. So we look like we're really part of the court and we're here to stay."

"I remain an advocate of the equal rights amendment."

"My rule was I will not answer a question that attempts to project how I will rule in a case that might come before the court."

"Every gal and every boy that's born alive is either a little liberal or else a little conservative."

"My mother graduated from high school at fifteen and went to work to support the family because the eldest son went to college."

"I'm not very good at promotion."

"I do think that being the second [female Supreme Court Justice] is wonderful, because it is a sign that being a woman in a place of importance is no longer extraordinary."

"Every constitution written since the end of World War II includes a provision that men and women are citizens of equal stature. Ours does not."

"We should learn to do our best for the sake of our communities and for the sake of those for whom we pave the way."

"The written argument endures. The oral argument is fleeting."

"I think we understand that for the Court to work well, we have to not only respect but genuinely like each other."

"People who think you could wave a magic wand and the legacy of the past will be over are blind."

"I think some of my colleagues' spicier lines are distracting. They draw attention away from what the justice is trying to say."

"My daughter, when she was in high school, she noticed the enormous difference between Daddy's cooking and Mommy's cooking. And decided that Mommy should be phased out of the kitchen altogether."

"Once it happened all the time that I would say something and there was no response. And then a man would say the same thing and people would say, 'Good idea.'"

"I see my advocacy as part of an effort to make the equality principle everything the founders would have wanted it to be if they weren't held back by the society in which they lived."

"This is a very intense job. It is by far the best and the hardest job I've ever had. And it takes a lot of energy and staying power to do it right."

"The number of women who have come forward as a result of the #MeToo movement has been astonishing. My hope is not just that it is here to stay, but that it is as effective for the woman who works as a maid in a hotel as it is for Hollywood stars."

"There are degrees of conduct, yes. But any time a woman is put in a position where she is inferior, she should not be afraid."

"The challenge is to make or keep our communities places where we can tolerate, even celebrate, our differences, while pulling together for the common good."

"If I am notorious, it is because I had the good fortune to be alive and a lawyer in the late 1960s."

"I was not,
100 percent sober."

"I had a life partner who thought my work was as important as his, and I think that made all the difference for me."

"Women belong in all places where decisions are being made."

"I would like to be remembered as someone who used whatever talent she had to do her work to the very best of her ability."

"When it's over, don't look back. Don't worry about things that are over and done. It's not productive to do that."